Focusing on Your Customer

Pocket Mentor Series

The Pocket Mentor Series offers immediate solutions to common challenges managers face on the job every day. Each book in the series is packed with handy tools, self-tests, and real-life examples to help you identify your strengths and weaknesses and hone critical skills. Whether you're at your desk, in a meeting, or on the road, these portable guides enable you to tackle the daily demands of your work with greater speed, savvy, and effectiveness.

Books in the series:

Focusing on Your Customer

Expert Solutions to Everyday Challenges

Harvard Business Review Press

Boston, Massachusetts

Library of Congress Cataloging-in-Publication Data

Focusing on your customer : expert solutions to everyday challenges.
        p. cm. — (Pocket mentor series)
    Includes bibliographical references.
    ISBN 978-1-4221-2975-3 (pbk. : alk. paper)   1. Customer relations.
2. Customer services.   3. Success in business.   I. Harvard Business School.
    HF5415.5.F63 2010
    658.8'12—dc22
                                              2010020122

Contents

Tips and Tools

the cost of replacing a specific employee, documenting feedback from customers, developing satisfaction goals for customers, improving a customer-related work process, and assessing service quality.

Test Yourself   73

A helpful review of concepts presented in this guide. Take it before and after you've read the guide, to see how much you've learned.

Answers to test questions   77

To Learn More   81

Further titles of articles and books if you want to go more deeply into the topic.

Sources for Focusing on Your Customer   89

Notes   91

For you to use as ideas come to mind.

Mentor's Message: Why Focus on Your Customer?

Most managers know that it's important to focus on their organization's customers. After all, without customers, a business wouldn't exist. But there's a far more specific reason for encouraging everyone in your group to focus on the customer: satisfying customers' needs translates directly into greater profitability for your enterprise.

How? When you and your team know who your firm's best customers are and what they want, you can deliver top-notch service to those customers. Your target customers respond by becoming loyal devotees of your company. Loyal customers buy more from the organization and are willing to pay more—enhancing revenues. At the same time, a company doesn't have to invest so much money in customer acquisition and marketing, so its costs decrease.

Pair increased revenues with decreased costs, and you get . . . profit!

This book helps you activate this cycle of success. You'll discover why customer loyalty is so important as an engine of profitability, how to target the right customers, how loyalty influences profitability in specific terms, and how to sharpen all employees' focus on target customers. You'll also learn valuable techniques for getting to know your best customers and their desires and then using that knowledge to deliver irresistible value to those customers. Throughout the book, you'll find a wealth of examples, tools, and exercises to help you master the information offered.

Focusing on your customer isn't just for the folks working in your company's marketing or sales department or the front-line employees who talk with customers every day. It's for everyone, no matter what role you play in your organization. This book helps you and your team achieve that focus—and start delivering even better results for your company.

James L. Heskett, Mentor

James L. Heskett has published extensively on customers, service, customer retention, employee capability, and profitability. He is Baker Foundation Professor Emeritus at Harvard Business School, where he has taught courses in service management, business policy, marketing, business logistics, and general management since 1965. Heskett is a coauthor of books including *The Ownership Quotient, The Service-Profit Chain,* and *Service Breakthroughs: Changing the Rules of the Game,* as well as a CD-ROM for managers titled *Service Success.* He is a consultant to management and a director of Limited Brands.

Focusing on Your Customer: The Basics

The "Three Rs" of Customer Loyalty

tudies show that the longer customers are loyal, the more profitable they become. Why? The answer has to do with what are known as the three Rs of customer loyalty: retention, related sales, and referrals.

Retention

The first R of customer loyalty is *retention*. An ongoing relationship with a customer creates a steady stream of revenue over time as the customer continues to buy products. The costs associated with marketing decline. In many cases, so do the costs of actually serving the customer, because he or she has become familiar with the company, its product lines, and its procedures.

> *Various estimates place the cost to attract new customers at five or more times the cost of retaining existing ones.*
> —James L. Heskett

Related sales

Loyal customers also generate *related sales*, or sales of new products and services to existing customers. The profit generated by related sales is greater than it is for selling to new customers. The forward-thinking company develops new products by listening to its loyal customers. Loyal customers are therefore more likely to buy because the new product has been designed to meet their needs, and because they already have a degree of faith in the company.

New sales to existing customers are less costly because they require less marketing, no new credit checks, less paperwork, and less time. Furthermore, loyal customers are often less sensitive to price than new customers.

Referrals

Positive *referrals* are the best kind of marketing—and they're free! Positive customer referrals are vital to profit and growth. Research suggests that satisfied customers are likely to tell five other people about a good experience, while dissatisfied customers are likely to tell eleven other people about a bad one. From your own experiences as a consumer, you probably know that personal referrals carry much more weight than traditional marketing does. And research has shown that when customers have been asked to provide a referral, most of them become more loyal.

The three Rs and your internal customers

The three Rs also come into play when your job involves serving internal customers—other individuals, groups, or teams within your organization. The longer a positive relationship with an internal customer lasts, the more you both accomplish together. As a long-term relationship with internal customers grows, the relationship becomes more and more effective, which in turn affects your company's profitability.

In a truly effective internal relationship, a synergy forms. Two groups within an organization can work together to develop new products or serve a customer in increasingly innovative and creative ways.

When marketing budgets ignore the three Rs

The figure "New versus loyal customers" represents a typical marketing budget. As you can see, only a small fraction of the entire budget is usually devoted to maintaining loyal customers.

Sadly, many companies today focus nearly all their energy and money on getting new customers. They promise low introductory rates and sign-up incentives, and, of course, they spend millions on marketing and advertising.

Moreover, the reward structure within many companies is geared almost exclusively to luring new customers into the fold.

FIGURE 1

New versus loyal customers

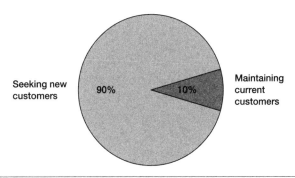

The biggest incentives often go to employees who bring in new customers, not to those employees who work hard at keeping loyal internal and external customers satisfied.

Marketing budgets like these are driven by the mistaken assumption that if you want to make a profit, you must increase market share. This traditional marketing approach focuses on the four Ps—product, price, promotional activity, and place (distribution channels). It leads to the notion that any customer is a good customer—which isn't accurate, as we'll see in the next section. And it neglects the importance of the three Rs.

Targeting the Right Customers

Not all customers are good customers; in fact, some customers are completely wrong for your company. In many companies, no more than 20 percent of customers generate 80 percent or more of the profit. Successful companies know exactly who their ideal customers are, and they focus their energy on creating products to please them, and only them.

Many customers are what you might call mercenaries. They're the kinds who, for example, change telephone services several times a year, lured by the cheapest rates and the biggest incentives. When the introductory offer runs out, so do they, long before they can ever be profitable.

A successful organization must concentrate on satisfying a targeted group of customers who place the highest value on the goods or services it offers. The company that does not make additional efforts to please these customers can stumble badly. Busy chasing the wrong customers, the company strays from what it does best, is more likely to encounter failure, and, in the process, alienates its most profitable customers.

Finding your target customers

Simply stated, your company's targeted customers should be those who will be loyal over time. Successful organizations determine who their target customers are and then do everything in their power to please and retain them. A well-defined target customer is a beacon for an organization to follow. Sometimes, an organization can determine its target customers by looking at the other side of the coin—in other words, by asking who it should *not* try to please. After all, no company can please everybody, and some customers are simply not worth having.

> *It takes months, even years to find a customer . . .*
> *and only seconds to lose one.*
> —Customer 101

For example, a successful U.S. insurance company was formed to serve a very specific target market: better-than-average drivers. Working in agricultural states, the company's agents were members of the community, constantly in touch with their customers, learning about what they needed and wanted. The company designed its marketing efforts to attract members of the target market and to keep loyal target customers happy. For instance, to reward customers' good driving practices, the firm gave discounts to good drivers at the end of three accident-free years.

Matching your target customers' expectations

Great companies remember that even target customers are *moving* targets; their expectations shift and evolve over time. Thus, service quality is not absolute, because it is determined by the customer, not by the service provider. And it varies from customer to customer. Consequently, excellent service-quality firms are those that can adapt their products and services to meet and exceed changing customer expectations.

What Would YOU Do?

Mercenary Customer—Or New Source of Profits?

CAROL HAD JUST STARTED as an account manager at Trident Telephony, a telecommunications company serving large corporations. She heard through the grapevine that PrimoTech, a major semiconductor firm, had just dumped its previous telephony services provider. Carol met with her boss, Rosco, to talk about the possibility of wooing PrimoTech over to Trident. "It'll be great for business!" she told him.

Rosco disagreed. "PrimoTech's notorious for getting bargain rates from one supplier and then jumping ship when the next big deal comes along," he said. "I doubt they'll stick around long enough to become profitable for us."

To make matters worse, Rosco knew that Carol's strategy for wooing PrimoTech would require moving resources from Trident's older, more profitable accounts to this new one. How could he prove to Carol that, at the very least, they should do everything possible to keep their loyal, profitable customers happy?

What would YOU do? The mentor will suggest a solution in *What You COULD Do.*

To illustrate, an automobile manufacturer with an extremely high loyalty rate noticed that it was losing customers. Managers contacted the defecting customers and asked why they were leaving. As it turned out, the customers were happy with the quality of the cars, but they were starting families and wanted bigger cars. Their expectations had changed. When the manufacturer responded by designing bigger cars, customer loyalty and sales improved.

What You COULD Do.

- Remember Rosco's concerns about how to explain to Carol the dangers of wooing PrimoTech?

Here's what the mentor suggests:

Rosco needs to show Carol that, while making individual sales is important, real profit comes from nourishing a relationship with a customer and watching it grow. He might sit down with Carol and explain the concept of the "lifetime value" of a customer and actually calculate the lifetime value of one of their clients. He could demonstrate how cultivating an ongoing relationship with a customer creates a steady revenue stream that requires less marketing to sustain. Loyal customers tend to buy related products, as well as generate additional revenue through positive referrals. Rosco might then help Carol calculate the potential revenue streams from an existing loyal client and from a new one.

Understanding How Customer Loyalty Affects Profitability

A s we've mentioned, customer loyalty has a direct impact on a company's profitability. To understand how this works, next we take a closer look at two important concepts: the lifetime value of a customer and the service-profit chain.

Calculating lifetime value of a customer

Once an organization targets its customers and begins to meet and exceed their expectations, customer satisfaction rises. Loyalty follows, bringing with it a significant and measurable impact on the bottom line.

In a recent study conducted across a wide range of service industries, experts found that relationships with typical customers grew increasingly more profitable over time in all cases, regardless of industry. Consider the following process:

1. **In year 1, the company acquires customers.** The organization must recoup these acquisition costs over the course of the relationship with those customers.

2. **Early on in the relationship, purchase and profit levels tend to be low.** But they create a foundation on which the company can build a longer-term customer relationship.

3. **Once a customer becomes familiar with a product or service, he or she is more likely to buy new products or services from that**

same company. The customer becomes less price-sensitive in making these purchases than with base product or service purchases. Because the company is selling its offerings to these customers at higher prices, its profit level increases.

4. **Having become knowledgeable about the company and its policies, the customer is less expensive to serve; therefore, the company's costs decrease (which further improves profitability).** Moreover, the truly loyal customer becomes an "apostle," someone who eagerly recommends the company to others, generating new business and greatly increasing profitability.

5. **The longer the customer relationship lasts, the more profitable it tends to become.** In one study of service firms, extending the customer relationship from five years to six years resulted in as much as a *25 percent to 85 percent increase in profitability*.

Why don't all companies pay more attention to their loyal customers? Because some don't appreciate how valuable these customers really are. Calculating the lifetime value of your customers can be an eye-opening experience. It can also help you build top management's support for customer-retention initiatives.

You can calculate lifetime value for any customer in any industry. Let's assume a business-to-business example: a small graphic design studio that buys software from a vendor. Here's what happens:

- **Year 1.** The owner of the design studio sees a television ad for new desktop layout software and makes a purchase. In this first year, the vendor doesn't make any money on this customer because the costs of acquiring and serving the customer are greater than the purchase price of the software program.

- **Year 2.** The customer, happy with the layout software, buys the upgrade (which has a higher profit margin) as well as a software program for drawing and illustrating. In addition, the studio owner refers the layout software to several independent graphic designers, one of whom buys the layout software.

- **Year 3.** The design studio buys a program for manipulating images and a clip-art library from the vendor. The first referral buys the drawing software and the layout software upgrade. Another referral purchases the layout software.

- **Year 4.** The design studio purchases a new upgrade to the layout software and an upgrade to the drawing software. The first referral purchases image-manipulation software and a clip-art library. The second referral purchases the drawing software and the layout software upgrade. In addition, two new referrals purchase the basic layout software.

- **Year 5.** The design studio buys new all-in-one software combining layout, illustration, and image-manipulation capabilities and purchases a different clip-art library. The first referral buys another upgrade to the layout software and an upgrade to the drawing software. The second referral buys image-manipulation software and a clip-art library. The two referrals from the past year each purchase the drawing software and the upgrade to the layout software.

TABLE 1

Calculating lifetime value, sample

	Year 1	Year 2	Year 3	Year 4	Year 5
Revenue from basic goods and services	$800	0	0	0	0
Revenue from new goods and services	0	$500 250	$500 200	$250 250	$3,000 200
Cost to (acquire and) serve	850	100	100	100	100
Referrals: Revenue from new loyal accounts	0	800	750 800	700 750 800 800	500 700 750 750
Profit	$(-)50	$1,450	$2,150	$3,450	$5,800

The purchases in years 1 through 5 that the design studio and its referrals made are tabulated in "Calculating lifetime value, sample." As you can see, the initial $800 purchase in year 1 leads to an additional *$12,850* of business from all sources in years 2 through 5.

"Steps for calculating the lifetime value of a customer" provides additional helpful information.

Appreciating the service-profit chain

Research across a wide variety of industries confirms that profitability and growth are strongly related to both employee and customer variables, such as:

- Employee capability

- Employee satisfaction

- Employee productivity

- Employees' ability to deliver good value to customers

- Customer satisfaction

- Customer loyalty

Steps for calculating the lifetime value of a customer

1. **Think about an average customer of your organization.** If your organization serves several very different market segments, you may want to choose customers from each segment and repeat this activity for each of those customers.

2. **Enter the number of sales transactions the average customer makes with your organization in the lifetime of his or her relationship with your company.** These transactions may be made in person or through a phone call, an order form, or a contract.

3. **Enter the average number of items or services that a customer purchases during each transaction.** If you provide service to customers on a contractual basis, write in the number *1* to represent one contract.

4. **Enter the average price per item that the customer pays.**

5. **Enter the average cost of acquiring a new customer.** A simple estimate of this cost would be the annual advertising expenses

divided by the number of new customers. Use the method for calculating marketing and advertising costs shown here, or develop your own.

Marketing and Advertising Cost Calculator

Annual marketing and advertising expenses: _____
Number of new customers per year: _____
Divide annual advertising and marketing expenses by the number of new customers you acquire in one year. (This is how much it costs you to acquire a new customer.)

_____

6. **Use this information with the calculating tool to determine the lifetime value of an average customer.** (See the tool "Calculating the Lifetime Value of a Customer" in the Tools section.)

7. **Repeat the calculations for a loyal, satisfied customer.** Compare the answer to that for a new customer. Remember, when you compare a new customer to a loyal customer, a loyal customer is more likely to:
   - Buy from you over a longer period.
   - Visit your organization more frequently.
   - Buy more during each interaction.
   - Be willing to pay more, especially for new products.
   - Refer other customers to you.

8. **Share the results of your calculations with all employees.** There's no better way to impress on them the importance of loyal customers and the value of customer satisfaction and retention.

These variables work together like links in a chain. In fact, experts have dubbed it the service-profit chain. Here's how it works: Employee capability—which a company builds by hiring the right people and giving them training, support, latitude, and rewards—promotes job satisfaction. When employees enjoy their work and believe they are making a difference, they tend to stay longer and become more productive and knowledgeable.

Such employee loyalty, in turn, creates greater customer satisfaction. After all, customers are more likely to be happy when they are being served by motivated employees who take the time to get to know their specific needs and circumstances. Not surprisingly, happy customers tend to buy more from the company and refer other customers to the company more frequently. Thus, customer satisfaction breeds customer loyalty. And there is a dramatic cause-and-effect relationship between customer loyalty and profitability: in some industries, a small percentage of a company's most valuable and loyal customers can account for more than half of total profitability.

The figure "The service-profit chain" depicts these connections.

FIGURE 2

The service-profit chain

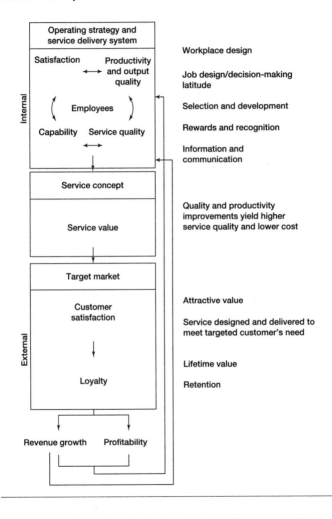

Sharpening Employees' Focus on Customers

M any organizations understand the need for training front-line workers to be polite, empathetic, and knowledgeable. But great front-line service is simply not enough. *Everyone* in the company should take responsibility for delivering the results the customer wants.

For example, a major airline subcontracted a shuttle service to fly passengers from a hub to the smaller airports in the region. Front-line workers were polite, industrious, and efficient. Unfortunately, the planes were never on time, if they took off at all. Flights were canceled almost continuously. Passengers constantly arrived hours or even a day late, frequently missing important events and meetings. Eventually, the poorly run shuttle service lost its contract and went out of business.

As this story shows, when capability is lacking anywhere, it compromises the company's ability to deliver what customers want. In the case of the airline, that was reliable transportation.

As a manager, you have the power and responsibility to strengthen the first link in the service-profit chain: employee capability.

Understanding the high cost of workforce turnover

Low employee job satisfaction and high turnover can create a downward spiral that causes sales and profits to plummet. For example, low job satisfaction can lead to a poor service attitude, which in turn can erode customer satisfaction.

Similarly, high turnover can disrupt continuity with customers; the resulting customer defection hurts the company's profits. Moreover, lower profits adversely affect training and job expectations. The consequence—low job satisfaction—starts the cycle of mediocrity over again. The figure "Cycle of mediocrity" captures these ideas.

Research suggests that employees place a high value in their jobs on *capability,* which can be translated roughly as the latitude and ability to deliver results to both internal and external customers. High perceived capability can, in turn, reduce employee turnover.

FIGURE 3

The cycle of mediocrity

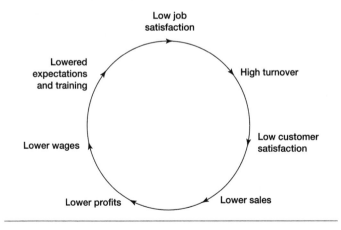

Successful organizations have lower employee turnover than their competitors. Even firms that typically have high turnover—for example, fast-food chains that hire low-skilled employees at minimal wages and provide them with minimal training—are beginning to understand that satisfied, long-term employees help build customer satisfaction and loyalty and cost less to manage. As a consequence, these companies are starting to question their long-standing assumptions.

The visible costs of bad hires and high employee turnover show up in related costs, such as additional recruiting and training expenses as well as lower productivity on the part of coworkers and managers. A broad range of hidden costs can be equally damaging. High turnover can have a negative impact on:

- The morale of other employees

- The quality of service provided

- Customer retention

- Productivity and profitability

Use the information you generate from calculating the cost of employee turnover in your own organization to help convince your colleagues that it makes economic sense to hire, train, support, and reward loyal employees.

Combating turnover

Most managers sincerely want to turn a cycle of mediocrity into a cycle of success. But good intentions often fall by the wayside due to the pressure of delivering high performance in the short term.

How can you, as a manager, help transform a cycle of mediocrity into a cycle of success? Start by selecting the right employees.

In simple terms, that means hiring for attitude and then training for skills. Skills (such as processing orders or developing products) can be taught, but it's difficult to train someone to have the right attitude toward customers. The most successful service organizations hire first for attitude and only secondly for skills. They train new hires in the skills they need for their jobs. "Tips for selecting the right people" offers helpful information on this point.

Everyone in your organization needs to have a customer-focused attitude. No one should be exempt, not even workers who spend little or no time in front of customers. For example, a talented but

Tips for selecting the right people

- Articulate the most important attributes and qualities of your most successful customer-service employees.
- Explain these attributes and qualities to job candidates. You'll encourage them to self-select into or out of a position. When candidates have a clear picture of the work and what's expected of them, they can better decide for themselves if they will thrive in the job. Candidates who are unsuited for the work are likely to select out of the job, saving you from making a bad hire.
- Consider a variety of creative recruiting techniques, such as involving customers in the selection of new hires.
- Ask your star performers to suggest job candidates. Winners attract winners.

egomaniacal software programmer can delay product releases and make life truly miserable for her teammates. If the programmer's attitude problems go unchecked, delays will continue, and your most highly skilled people will find jobs with a competitor.

To avoid this kind of scenario, make sure that new employees receive training in the skills and tools they need to perform their jobs well. Training should include an appropriate mix of interpersonal and technical skills. Training in interpersonal skills is vital for employees who spend a great deal of time interacting with external customers. But it's also important for anyone serving internal customers—others within an organization—and anyone participating in a team.

Of course, training takes time and money. Yet organizations that invest in employee development win payoffs in the form of reduced employee turnover, improved service quality, and increased productivity. Result? Increased customer satisfaction and loyalty.

In the pages that follow, we describe some additional ways you can combat turnover among your customer-facing employees.

Provide tools and support. Once you've hired winners, give them the chance to "win" on the job. Provide them with the tools and support they need to excel in their roles, such as technology, information systems, workplace design, and service facilities. They will perform better and feel better about their jobs. Your reward? Increased employee loyalty, which translates into increased customer loyalty.

Without adequate support systems, even the best hires cannot deliver the results and service they want to give customers. "Tips for providing tools and support" provides some helpful suggestions on this front.

Tips for providing tools and support

- Think about your own group. Does it have the systems in place that enable it to succeed? What are the barriers?
- Think about your external and internal customers. What are their common complaints? What do customers want that your tools and systems do not support?
- Be sure that any new support systems you consider are in line with your organization's strategy. For example, will the new systems help you better deliver the results that your customers truly want? How will these systems affect the way work is currently performed? Will the new systems require training?

Allow latitude—within limits. Once you've hired the right people, trained them to make sure they have the right skills, and provided them with effective support, give them expanded latitude to deliver value to customers. Latitude gives these employees the power and responsibility to make quick decisions and to recover decisively from mistakes. An organization benefits from capable employees' judgment and decision-making capabilities.

By contrast, micromanagement is demeaning and frustrating to capable employees. They resent being treated as incompetent, and they become dissatisfied with their work. Their productivity declines. The most valuable employees will find work somewhere else.

Still, latitude must be accompanied by limits. Determining the right latitude and limits depends on the circumstances. Greater employee latitude is especially beneficial in jobs that are difficult to supervise or jobs that require a great deal of interaction combined with a need for quick service recovery (or resolution after something goes wrong in serving a customer). "Tips for granting latitude within limits" provides additional recommendations.

Tips for granting latitude within limits

- To determine whether you've given your employees enough latitude, ask them if they feel micromanaged. Ask them what decisions they feel they could be making that they are not allowed to make now. Determine which processes or procedures impede their ability to make decisions.
- Set limits in one of two ways: clearly define what employees can and cannot do, or define a core set of required standards. As long as employees meet those standards, they have freedom to do what it takes to meet customers' needs.
- Make sure that the latitudes and limits for your work group enable employees to meet external and internal customer needs and deliver the results and service value that customers want.

Reward results. Recognize and reward your people for their ongoing contributions to high-quality customer service. Tie rewards directly to goals. Rewards should reflect the culture and values of your organization and should reinforce what most motivates your employees. While it may be easier to measure and evaluate effort, remember that your objective is to deliver results to customers. Reward employees who achieve results rather than merely make an effort. See "Tips for rewarding results" for additional guidelines.

Tips for rewarding results

- Determine the results and goals—the more specific and measurable, the better—that you want employees to achieve.
- Align rewards with the organization's mission and culture. For example, if getting people to work together cooperatively is a company goal, don't set up a highly competitive reward structure.
- Look for creative ways to recognize individuals or groups. For example, establish programs in which awards are given by peers or even by customers. Or, share profits with those who participated in generating them.
- Announce achievements in company newsletters, on bulletin boards, on your corporate intranet, or in a companywide e-mail. Let everyone know who succeeded and why.

Getting to Know Your Customers

The relationship between a loyal customer and successful organization is a dynamic, ongoing process fueled by constant two-way communication and responsiveness.

The difference between average and excellent organizations is how effectively management obtains feedback from customers, listens to it, communicates the information internally, and acts on it. Instead of telling customers what to do through constant advertising and hard-sell pitches, companies must focus on listening. Every organization already has built-in mechanisms for getting feedback, but many don't use these mechanisms well. By understanding these mechanisms, as well as learning about customers through observation, companies can strengthen those all-important organization–customer bonds.

Obtaining feedback from customers

Successful companies strive to continually exceed their target customers' expectations. To accomplish this, they listen to target customers to find out what products and services they want, and how they want those offerings delivered. But as we've noted, customers are moving targets; their expectations are constantly changing. For this reason, organizations need as many opportunities to hear and respond to customer feedback as they can find. Every organization has *listening posts,* places where employees hear customer feedback. Organizations can create both formal and informal ways to find out how customers are doing.

All tools that measure feedback are best used in an atmosphere of trust. They should be used to gather useful information as a way to improve products and services, not as weapons or methods for assigning blame or punishing people. And all tools should measure both positive and negative feedback from customers.

> *All the smiles in the world aren't going to help you if your*
> *product or service is not what the customer wants.*
> —Carl Sewell and Paul Brown

Listening posts include:

- **Web sites.** Your company's Web site offers an excellent arena for obtaining customer feedback quickly and easily. Make the most of e-mail functionality by soliciting general feedback prominently on your site and posting e-mail addresses for designated contact people. Scan bulletin boards on your site or look at those of competitors to find out what people are saying about your products or services.

- **Social media.** Monitor what people are saying about your company and its offerings through social media sites such as Facebook and Twitter as well as through consumers' Web sites and blogs.

- **Audits.** Audits take many forms. Perhaps the most popular among them is "mystery shopping." To use this type of audit, have designated mystery shoppers make actual visits to your company's retail or other business sites, call its customer service providers, or purchase and use its products or services—and then report on their experiences. Many people believe that mystery shopping offers a high degree of objectivity, although employees can regard it as unfair or even as "spying" if it's not evenly conducted to identify areas for improvement.

- **Market research.** Many large corporations hire market research firms to do extensive studies that explore consumers' demographics, lifestyles, buying habits, preferences, and buying patterns. Small businesses may not be able to commission such extensive studies, but they can get data from the Small Business Administration.

- **Focus groups.** There are many kinds of focus groups, from small, informal meetings to elaborate, carefully orchestrated sessions. An informal group of customers from a target market can help your company test an initial product idea, design, or concept. As the product develops, the company may begin to conduct more geographically expansive, professionally organized focus groups. Such groups are excellent for testing products and services, but the results are often contradictory, which can send an unfocused company into disarray.

- **The ordering process.** One of the most overlooked listening posts is a company's ordering process. Whether an order is taken in person, over the phone, or on the Web, you can gain valuable information from customers by asking the right questions and listening carefully at this contact point.

- **Satisfaction cards.** Most service industries give customers a chance to fill out guest satisfaction cards. Today, these cards are prevalent in industries like food and lodging, health care, and automotive care.

- **Surveys.** A well-designed survey can help you determine what you are doing to deliver the greatest satisfaction, or lack of it. More elaborate than a satisfaction card, a survey measures many areas. Sometimes a company will follow up a written survey with a phone interview. Managers can use information gathered from surveys to replicate the most successful strategies and solve any problem areas.

- **The customer service process.** Complaints that arise in the course of serving a customer should be carefully studied and responded to promptly. At one successful hotel chain, when a customer complains, the complaint is noted on a guest incident form and entered that day into a database to notify other hotel personnel. This practice helps employees know that the guest may need special attention.

- **Follow-up satisfaction calls.** Recently, many organizations have established a follow-up satisfaction call as another customer listening post. More elaborate than a card, but less involved than a comprehensive survey, the follow-up call is a personal, brief phone call that takes place shortly after a transaction. A representative calls the customer to make sure that everything is okay and to ask a few, simple questions about the products and services involved.

A well-trained representative can spot service recovery problems before they begin and can reveal more general information about what the target customer values or does not value. (See "Steps for achieving excellent service recovery.") For example, a major optical company calls customers about a week after they buy a pair of glasses. They check to make sure that the glasses fit properly and invite the customer in for a follow-up fitting. At that time, representatives also ask a few other, brief questions that measure satisfaction. This extra service distinguishes this optical company from its competitors and helps ensure repeat business.

Follow-up calls are also excellent marketing tools, because they help establish a feeling of trust between the company and the customer. A follow-up satisfaction call should be a sincere effort to ask about and provide service. The company should not use it to sell. If the caller uses a satisfaction call as a trick to push additional products, the customer will almost certainly become annoyed.

Steps for achieving excellent service recovery

1. **Find out what the problem is.**
   - Listen carefully to the customer's explanation of the problem.
   - Ask questions to clarify.
   - Paraphrase to be sure you understand the problem.
2. **Find out what the customer expects you to do about it.**
   - Listen to what the customer wants you to do about the problem.

- If you can meet the customer's expectations, offer assurances that you will solve the problem.

3. **Take personal responsibility for solving the problem.**
    - Offer to help.
    - Don't pass the problem along to someone else.
    - Know the policies of your organization.
    - Explain the options calmly.

4. **Go out of your way to make the customer comfortable.**
    - If you know that a problem may take a while to solve, do whatever you can to make the customer comfortable during the wait.
    - If on the phone, don't leave a person on hold for more than two minutes. Instead, offer to call back.
    - In a face-to-face situation, suggest the customer wait in a more comfortable area, or come back in an hour.
    - Offer lunch, coffee, or magazines—anything to show that you care and that you will solve the problem.

5. **Maintain an objective frame of mind.**
    - If a customer grows angry, don't take it personally. The person is angry at the problem, not at you.
    - So just listen. Let the person get his or her feelings out.

6. **Stay positive and calm.**
    - Apologize for the difficulty, even when it was not your fault.
    - Don't blame others for the problem.
    - Never tell an external customer that the problem is something that always happens.

7. **Resolve the problem quickly.**
    - Think resourcefully. Try to determine the fastest and most effective way to solve the problem.

- Offer reasonable alternatives if you can't give the customer exactly what he or she wants.
- If you need to get someone else involved, explain the problem so the customer does not have to repeat it. And stay involved, even when someone else is helping.

8. **Follow through.**
   - At a later time, make sure the problem was solved to the customer's satisfaction.
   - Never ask the customer whether the problem was solved or what happened. You should know these answers.
   - Send a letter of apology, a gift, or premiums such as coupons, a free item, or additional service.

9. **Look at the big picture.**
   - Determine if the problem is a recurring one. If so, figure out ways to prevent it from happening again.
   - Work with others to find out how they solve similar problems.
   - Try to put a dollar cost on poor recovery.

10. **Look for common sources of problems in the recovery process itself.** For example, the source of the problem may be one of the following:
    - Inappropriate selection of people to handle recovery.
    - Inadequate internal support systems (information and other) to do the job.
    - Poor training.
    - Insufficient latitude (within limits) allowed by management to deliver results to customers.
    - Inadequate recognition and reward for good service recovery.

Observing customers

Obtaining customer feedback through listening posts is crucial. So is watching your customers while they are using your product or service. There's simply no substitute for direct observation of your customers. So, get out into the field with qualified observers and see how your customers use your product in real life. You'll find out what they like, what they don't like, and how they would improve your product or service. You'll be surprised to hear things you never even thought of.

For example, at a major photocopying company, observers in the field found that copy machines were usually placed in storerooms. People frequently stood on the machine to reach the highest shelves. Knowing this, product designers created a copy machine strong enough to support a person's weight.

When you go into the field, bring along observers with different backgrounds and skills. A diversity of perspectives can provide valuable information. "Steps for observing customers and designing solutions" offers additional guidance on this topic.

Steps for observing customers and designing solutions

1. **Observe customers.** The best way to capture the most important aspects of the environment and people you choose to observe is to send out a small team. Each team member should have expertise in a different discipline. An engineer, for example,

may notice mechanical interactions, while a designer may see space and forms.

The people the team is observing should be carrying out normal routines—playing, eating, relaxing, or working at home or at the office. For some products or services, team members may conduct their observations unobtrusively. For example, by simply planting themselves in a public setting where people are going about their normal routines, team members can watch behaviors systematically.

2. **Capture the data.** Observers can capture the best data through silent observation, but they may want to ask a few open-ended questions, such as:
   – "Why are you doing that?"
   – "Please describe to me your most recent or most memorable _____ [the activity that is your focus, for example, fishing, making a bank deposit, installing software]."

   Observers may carry a list of questions to prompt their own observations, such as, "What problems is the user encountering?"

   Video, audio recordings, still photographs, drawings, and notes can help the observers capture subtle body language that may convey important information and store it for future review and analysis.

3. **Collate and analyze the data.** Present the data collected (including photos, drawings, videos, audiotapes) to colleagues and/or customers who did not take part in the observation. These individuals will see different things than the observation team did. As they observe the data your observation team

collected, ask them if they see any problems or opportunities or have any other comments. Use the data to identify possible problems or needs of those observed.

4. **Brainstorm solutions.** Heed the five rules of brainstorming: defer judgment, build on the ideas of others, hold one conversation at a time, stay focused on the topic, and encourage wild ideas. You may want to include some customers, noncustomers, or competitor's customers in the brainstorming session.

    Provide any supporting infrastructure needed. This can be as low-tech as flip charts or a table covered in paper used for doodling and note taking. At the end of a session, members can tear off the best ideas and take them with them to ponder.

5. **Narrow the field of solutions.** Determine your criteria for choosing solutions. For example:
    - What functions are essential (from your customers' point of view) and what are "nice to have"?
    - What criteria are determined by the company's values?
    - What are your cost constraints?
    - What are your size or shape constraints (for a product)?
    - Within what time frame must you complete the project?
    - In what ways must the product or service be compatible with existing products or services?

    Given these constraints, determine which solutions are most feasible.

6. **Develop prototypes of possible solutions.** Prototypes clarify the concept of the new product or service for the development

team. (Or they may show the lack of clarity in your product or service.)

- Prototypes enable the team to place its concept in front of other individuals whose functions are not formally represented on the team.
- Prototypes can stimulate reaction and foster discussion with potential customers.
- Sometimes two prototypes are used when demonstrating a product—one that shows function but not form, and one that shows the physical appearance of the intended product but doesn't work.
- Simulations can be useful prototypes. Role playing can also be used as a prototype of particular behaviors or actions, such as a service product.

Delivering Irresistible Value to Your Customers

Once you've sharpened employees' focus on target customers and gotten to know your customers through gathering feedback from them and observing them, you can use the information to deliver irresistible value to customers. There are four keys for doing this: understanding the customer value equation, developing satisfaction goals for profitable customers, establishing customer-friendly processes, and designing customer listening posts. In the pages that follow, we look at each of these in turn.

Understanding the customer value equation

What is value? Think about your own experience as a customer. How do you determine what's most important to you? Did you get the results you expected when you purchased and used a product or service? Were the results delivered the way you wanted them? Did the supplier make it convenient for you to acquire the product or service you wanted? Was the price what you were hoping for?

A calculation known as the *customer value equation* factors in all these considerations to arrive at the measure of value that the customer perceives. But before we look at the calculation itself, let's examine in greater detail each factor that goes into it.

- **Results.** Customers buy results they value. They don't buy products and services. A customer buys a prescription to deal with an ailment. The result is a cure. A customer fills the car with gas. The result is transportation. A customer buys a dinner at a fancy restaurant. The result is a pleasant evening of fine dining and entertainment.

- **Process quality.** This is the way the product or service is delivered. Process quality is a combination of such factors as dependability, timeliness, and a professional attitude on the part of company representatives.

- **Price and access costs.** Price is only one factor in the ultimate cost of the product or service to the customer. When customers consider price, they also add in the access costs. A cheaper product that requires that the customer drive sixty miles to obtain it may not be worth the price. On the other hand, the added cost of overnight delivery may be well worth it to a customer who wants convenience.

The customer value equation can be expressed as follows:

Results + process quality/price + customer access costs

Developing satisfaction goals for profitable customers

You've listened to the customer. You understand what the customer wants and expects. You know what the customer values. Now you have enough information to develop satisfaction goals for your profitable customers. In addition to sources you have already developed, consider using:

- Service criteria

- Informal polls of employees who deal with customers

What Would YOU Do?

Things Aren't So Easy at Easy Order, Inc.

ASY ORDER, INC., a mail-order company, has seen its revenues settle into a holding pattern. Market research shows that Easy Order isn't gaining or losing customers, and the existing customers are purchasing products at a steady level.

Arnold manages Easy Order's marketing group. To stimulate revenues, Easy Order has approved a small increase in the marketing budget—just enough for one marketing campaign. Arnold and his group decide to use the increase to target established, loyal customers. Their marketing initiative—dubbed "Lift Loyalty"—is companywide. The goal is to increase customer loyalty and encourage loyal customers to buy more products. Employees on the front line are encouraged to look for ways to increase loyalty and sales.

Arnold has lunch with a colleague, Brenda, who manages customer orders. Her group takes orders over the phone and through the company's Web site. Brenda tells Arnold that she's worried: her front-line employees are growing frustrated and disgruntled. In fact, she recently lost two employees. One complained she "couldn't do a good job." The other said, "It's not enough just to tell us to *look for* ways to increase customer loyalty." To support the marketing initiative, Brenda knows she needs to turn things around—quickly.

But how? Should she ask Arnold to reduce the pressure on her people from the new campaign? What about giving her people more responsibility and autonomy to help customers? Should she bring in new people with the specific skills needed to carry out the campaign? It all seems so complicated …

What would YOU do? The mentor will suggest a solution in *What You COULD Do*.

- Informal polls of customers
- Informal polls of supervisors
- Experience and judgment
- Common sense (often overlooked)

The table, "Developing satisfaction goals—examples," sheds additional light on this subject.

Goals should consist of factors that influence the satisfaction of your profitable customers. Remember, some people will only be satisfied with a product or service that costs them less than what it costs you to produce. Obviously, pleasing those customers will not be profitable for your company.

Establishing customer-friendly processes

Many problems that arise in serving customers stem from clumsy processes. For example, hidden costs or deadlines hinder delivery of a service. Customers wait too long on the phone for help. A billing process is complicated and confusing.

TABLE 2

Developing satisfaction goals—examples

Target area	Sample goal
Style of interaction	We will treat every customer with respect.
Timing	We will respond to every customer within five minutes.
Attitude	We will explain our product features and functions in the language of the customer, not in the language of our organization.
Communication	We will end every interaction with a customer by asking if there is anything else we can do.
Policies and procedures	We will increase the amount of petty cash available. Internal customers will no longer have to pay for their own expenses and then be reimbursed.
Employee latitude	Following company guidelines, employees will be able to authorize checks without the approval of a manager.
Customer retention	Over the next year, we will increase retention of profitable customers from our current rate of 50% to 65%.

Research has shown that there are five generic influences of service process quality that can negatively affect customers:

- **Dependability.** Did the service provider do what he said he would do?

- **Responsiveness.** Was the service provided in a timely manner?

- **Authority.** Did the service provider help the customer feel confident about the service-delivery process?

- **Empathy.** Did the service provider demonstrate the ability to see things from the customer's perspective?

- **Tangible evidence.** Is it irrefutably clear that a service has been provided?

Keep these influences in mind when problems arise. Chances are, the problems will be linked to one or more of the generic influences. To identify process problems, begin by mapping out every step of the service process. Examine each step by asking what the purpose of the step is and how it adds value to the service or product. Explore the source of each problem step. "Steps for mapping a service process" provides additional guidance on how to do this.

Steps for mapping a service process

1. **Choose a service process that many employees perform—one that has a strong impact on customer satisfaction and is prone to problems.**
2. **List the activities involved in the process.** Use a separate note, index card, or sheet of paper for each activity.
3. **Arrange the activities in the sequence in which they occur.** Indicate how long it takes to complete each step.
4. **Transfer this information to a work process map.** Add or subtract levels as appropriate.
    - List people involved down the left (vertical) side of the map.

- Divide the horizontal axis of the map into appropriate segments of time, such as hours or days.
- Arrange the work activities in sequence from left to right across the map with arrows to indicate the flow. You may find it helpful to represent each activity with a numbered box and include a legend below to name and describe them.

5. **Brainstorm with the group to determine fail points.** Fail points are:
   - Inefficiencies
   - Unnecessary steps
   - Lost time
   - Any factor that inhibits timely, high-quality products or services

   You'll see that the two dimensions of the map (vertical and horizontal) provide new insights regarding cost and customer satisfaction.

6. **Study the map from different perspectives.** Put yourself in your customers' shoes. Then ask again how you can change the work process to eliminate fail points and to deliver better service.

Designing effective customer listening posts

Companies can design the questions asked at listening posts to find out whether the products and services satisfied customers buy are continuing to meet their needs. Responses to these questions can shed light on whether you should adapt existing products to respond to new needs or add new services to respond to consumers' changing lifestyles.

For example, when a leading provider of baked goods saw sales begin to level off, managers decided to find out why. By asking questions, they learned that most loyal customers were growing older and becoming more concerned about fat and cholesterol in their diets. These customers were no longer satisfied with the company's products or delivery. They stopped buying the company's baked goods because the product line no longer met their needs. Managers discovered that if the firm were to offer low-fat products, the loyal customers would be happy to buy them. By listening to their most devoted customers, the company determined that it should offer new products, which have since become very successful.

Companies must design and use listening posts to measure customers' satisfaction, of course. But they can also use them to measure factors that will gauge the possible defection of satisfied customers. See "Steps for developing listening posts" and "Steps for improving listening posts" for more information on this.

Customer satisfaction is not a surrogate for customer retention. While it may seem intuitive that increasing customer satisfaction will increase retention and therefore profits, the facts are contrary. Between 65 percent and 85 percent of customers who defect say they were satisfied or very satisfied with their former supplier.
—Frederick Reichheld

Steps for developing listening posts

1. **Determine your listening posts.** List points at which your organization receives customer feedback—for example, sales representatives, marketing research results, telephone representatives, customer service representatives, or servers.

2. **Interview employees to find out what feedback they are receiving.**

3. **Organize the feedback.** Categorize the significant types of feedback from each listening post. Feedback can include such things as suggestions for new product features, confusion about service terms, or annoyance about waiting for product delivery.

4. **Determine the current use of the feedback.** Find out how employees are using feedback. Are they using it to make product improvements or to create better service agreement instructions? Do they talk about the feedback and then ignore it?

5. **Decide how you *should* use feedback.** Take action to use valuable feedback. Involve your employees in coming up with ways to make feedback more useful by converting it into data they can use in their jobs.

Steps for improving listening posts

1. **Review the feedback you are receiving.**
2. **Look at the timing of information you get.** Is the information coming in at the right time? Can you get the feedback earlier? You can use many listening posts more proactively to prevent problems before they occur.
3. **Decide what you want to know about customer behavior.** There are information gaps about customers in every organization. Why are customers loyal? Why do satisfied customers defect? Why do new customers come here? Brainstorm the big-picture information the organization needs about retention, defection, and overall satisfaction and ways of getting it.
4. **Design ways to use listening posts to find out what you want to know.** Develop questions to uncover patterns in customer behavior. For example, when an order is taken, representatives in many organizations ask new customers, "How did you hear about us?" When properly recorded and tracked, the answer to this simple question is invaluable. It helps assess advertising and marketing efforts, as well as the rate of referrals.
5. **Establish a process to build in new questions at key listening posts.** People asking questions must understand why they are asking the questions, and they must have an easy-to-follow process to gather the information. Simple forms, brief weekly meetings, and informal chats are all ways to be sure that people are asking good questions at the right time.

6. **Assess the need for new listening posts.** Many organizations are adding a follow-up satisfaction call to the listening posts they already have. Once you have redesigned your current listening posts, ask yourself if you need to add other types.

What You COULD Do.

Remember Brenda's question about how to address her employees' frustrations?

Here's what the mentor suggests:

If you recall, one of Brenda's employees said she "couldn't do a good job." This suggests that Brenda's team members likely need more latitude to make on-the-spot decisions and take immediate action to support the marketing initiative. Brenda's direct reports are in the best position to have a positive impact on customer loyalty. Also, employees who can "make a difference" tend to enjoy their work more, stay longer, and become even more productive. Research shows that employees place a high value on latitude— the freedom to make decisions and the ability to deliver results to customers.

Tips and Tools

Tools for Focusing on Your Customer

CALCULATING THE LIFETIME VALUE OF A CUSTOMER

Use this worksheet to calculate the lifetime value of one of your customers.

Customer name:

Basic formula

Estimate # of customer transactions in lifetime	Number of purchases per visit	Average price per purchase ($)	Cost to acquire a customer ($)	Lifetime value of a customer ($)
[ ] ×	[ ] ×	[ ] −	[ ] =	[ ]

Projected formula, 5-year period

	Revenue (Include gross revenue generated)	Cost (Calculate costs to service this customer, including marketing, and costs of making and delivering product or service.)	Referrals (Add net value of referred accounts.)	Profit ($)
Year 1	[ ] −	[ ] +	[ ] =	[ ]
Year 2	[ ] −	[ ] +	[ ] =	[ ]
Year 3	[ ] −	[ ] +	[ ] =	[ ]
Year 4	[ ] −	[ ] +	[ ] =	[ ]
Year 5	[ ] −	[ ] +	[ ] =	[ ]
			Total:	[ ]

Use this worksheet to think through what your customers value, which you can think of as an equation. The service value as determined by the customer is equal to the results received times how the service is delivered, in relation to the price of the service times any costs for acquiring the service. The values in the equation are relative, since different customers often want different things, or the same customer may want different things at different times. For example, you may value convenience and the opportunity to save time more in one situation, or price in another. Think through how you can leverage the factors in this equation to add value to the customer, and enhance your business.

What customers value. *Fill in this equation with descriptions of what your customers value. You do not have to use a specific dollar amount in the price category, but could use descriptive terms such as high, low, competitive pricing, every day low price (EDLP), premium, discounted, and so forth.*

Results		**Delivery/Process Quality**
What results do your customers want?		*How do they want the results delivered?*
	×	

Look at the above in relationship to the factors below.

Price		**Access Costs**
What price are they willing to pay for the product or service?		*What costs are they willing to incur to get the product or service?*
	×	

Value summary

What are the key customer value equations most prevalent in your business?

What factors or situations could affect these equations? Which ones can you alter or control?

How can you leverage these factors to increase the value of your service (or product) to the customer?
For example, increase convenience while keeping price the same.

CALCULATING EMPLOYEE TURNOVER

This worksheet is fairly general. Estimate the data and then enter it in the columns below.

Factors	Average employee	New employee	Difference
Revenue per week			
Cost per week			
Contribution per week			

Average estimated cost to hire new employee	
Average estimated cost to train new employee	
Estimate revenues lost by vacant position	
Cost of on-the-job support, including supervision provided	
Cost of single employee turnover (*Add hiring, training, revenue, job support costs*)	
Number of replacement employees per year	
Annual cost of employee turnover (*Cost of employee times number of replacement employees per year*)	

CALCULATING THE COST OF REPLACING A SPECIFIC EMPLOYEE

Use this form to calculate the cost of employee turnover in one position or salary range per year. Calculate costs for replacement employees only. Do not calculate costs for employees hired to fill new positions.

Position:	Salary level:
Hiring costs	
Direct costs to hire one new employee	
Advertising	
Average fee to employment agencies, placement firm	
Sign-on bonus	
Referral bonuses to other employees	
Travel and expenses (include your expenses and money you reimburse to prospective candidate)	
Other direct costs	
Total direct costs to hire	
Indirect costs to hire one new employee	
Estimate the costs incurred by having all current employees perform the following activities related to a new hire:	
Interviewing (costs of current employees at all levels of interviewing, from initial phone call through final interviews)	
Checking references	
Lost revenue (include costs of time spent away from actual jobs)	
Miscellaneous indirect costs (phone, copy, fax)	
Total indirect costs to hire	
Training costs	
Direct costs to train one new employee	
Time spent by person/people directly responsible for training new hire to do job. Cost per hour times number of hours	
Cost per participant of general training programs, training materials, seminars for new hires	

Travel and expenses per participant for above	
Other direct costs	
Total direct costs to train	
Indirect costs to train one new employee	
Estimate the time spent by all current employees who are involved in training a new candidate:	
General training in company technology and procedures, processes, etc.	
On-the-job training costs before employee becomes fully productive	
Total indirect costs to train	
Lost productivity costs (*note: this section applies to any job that has sales or productivity measures that can be converted to dollar amounts*)	
Indirect costs incurred until employee is performing at expected level	
Lost revenues for the time the position is vacant (multiply the revenues a typical employee generates per month by the number of the months the position will be vacant)	
Lost revenue during the time the employee is getting up to speed (calculate the difference between the revenues a new employee generates and what an existing employee generates during the training and transition period)	
Total lost productivity costs	
Total cost of replacing a single employee	
Annual cost of employee turnover	
To calculate the annual cost of employee turnover, multiply the cost of replacing one employee times the number of replacements each year.	

CUSTOMER FEEDBACK CHART

Use this form to record data when you are evaluating listening posts and feedback pathways. The completed chart can guide the improvement of current listening posts and the development of new ones.

Listening post	Types of feedback	Current destination	Desired destination	Current use(s) of feedback
Example *Customer Service*	*Complaint: product malfunction; customer wants to return the product*	*Returns Dept.*	*Report of returns to Returns Dept., Product Group, Marketing, Sales*	*Improve product performance and development.*

Improving the effectiveness of listening posts

Question	Response
1. *Are some current listening posts collecting valuable data that is not being forwarded and used effectively in the organization? What? Why not?*	
2. *How do you want the feedback to be used?*	
3. *Are there new listening posts that should be set up to collect additional data?*	

DEVELOPING SATISFACTION GOALS FOR CUSTOMERS

Use this worksheet to brainstorm goals in target areas.

Target area	Satisfaction goal
Style of interaction *How do you interact with your customers now?* *How could you make it more personal?* *More informative?* *More effective?* *More fun?*	
Timing *How promptly do you respond to your customers' requests?* *Could your response time be faster?*	
Attitude *What attitude do you express to each customer?* *Can your attitude be more focused?* *Helpful?* *Concerned?*	
Communication *How do you communicate with your customer?* *Do you listen effectively?* *Do you ask the right questions?* *Do you speak clearly?*	
Policies and procedures *What policy or procedure most annoys your customers?* *What policy or procedure most frequently gets between you and your customer?* *How can you change it?*	
Employee latitude *Do employees have the ability to take initiative and solve problems instantly?* *In what areas do they wish they had more freedom to solve problems on their own?*	

IMPROVING A WORK PROCESS

Choose a work process that many employees perform, that has a strong impact on customer satisfaction, and that is prone to problems. With a representative group, break the process down into a series of sequential activities or steps, then dig deeper to uncover improvement opportunities or "fail points." Fail points are inefficiencies, unnecessary steps, lost time, or any other factor that inhibits timely, quality products or services from being produced or delivered to the customer. When you've identified a problem, ask, "Why does this happen?" Continue repeating the question to probe for cause-effect relationships. This will help ensure that the work process improvement isn't just fixing a symptom, but the problem.

Work process:

Activities	Value	Problem	Solutions
List each step or activity in the process, in sequence.	*Does this add value for the customer? Organization?*	*Are there fail points here? Why? Improvement opportunities?*	*Brainstorm solutions or improvements.*
1.			
2.			
3.			
4.			
5.			
6.			
7.			

SERVICE QUALITY ASSESSMENT

Use or adapt this form to survey your internal or external customers on the level of service they received from your organization. You can modify the questions within this document for a service or manufacturing industry, or specifically tailor the questions to your business.

Service quality assessment
Please use a rating scale from 1 to 5 to indicate how satisfied you are with the level of service you received when you placed your order. On the left side, please rate the importance of each item to you. Then, on the right side, indicate your degree of satisfaction with our performance. Use NA if the item is not applicable to you.

Importance *Low High* 1 2 3 4 5		Satisfaction *Low High* 1 2 3 4 5
	Speed with which your call is answered	
	Helpful, courteous customer service or sales representative	
	Representative takes time to answer all questions	
	Ability to speed up an order in a rush situation	
	Speed with which you received your order	
	Good condition of order upon arrival	
	Ease of returning a product	
	Ability to trace an order	
	Fast and effective problem resolution	
	Representative knowledgeable about product	
	Representative treated you like a valued customer	
	Other:	

How can we improve our service to you?
Please describe below your suggestions for how we can improve the quality of our service to you.

Please return this form:

Via e-mail to:

Via mail to:

Via fax to:

We thank you for your business and look forward to serving you again.

Test Yourself

This section offers ten multiple-choice questions to help you identify your baseline knowledge of customer focus.

Answers to the questions are given at the end of the test.

1. What are the "three Rs" of customer loyalty?

    a. Revenues, retention, and returns.

    b. Retention, related sales, and referrals.

    c. Recognition, reward, and research.

2. How much does the *typical* marketing budget devote to seeking new customers versus maintaining current customers?

    a. 90 percent to seeking new customers; 10 percent to maintaining current customers.

    b. 20 percent to seeking new customers; 80 percent to maintaining current customers.

    c. 50 percent to seeking new customers; 50 percent to maintaining current customers.

3. Which of the following statements is accurate about target customers?

    a. Their expectations remain stable over time.

b. They change companies to find the best prices and capture big incentives.

  c. They place the highest value on the goods or services your company offers.

4. Which mutually reinforcing connections form the "service-profit chain"?

  a. Innovative services and products, attractive pricing, and incentives for customer loyalty.

  b. Employee capability, job satisfaction, and productivity; employee loyalty; customer satisfaction and loyalty.

  c. A healthy marketing budget, higher-than-expected profits, and deep understanding of customer needs.

5. High employee turnover can harm the service-profit chain by disrupting continuity with customers, increasing customer defections, and reducing profitability. What's the *first* step you would take to reduce employee turnover?

  a. Take stock of which skills your employees need to provide excellent customer service and provide the training needed to close any skills gaps.

  b. Provide your current best employees with incentives and recognition to ensure that they stay with the company.

  c. Hire people with a customer-focused attitude, with the idea that you'll train them for the skills they'll need in their jobs.

6. Which of the following is the *best* step to take when trying to support the service-profit chain for your department or group?

   a. Ensure that the front-line employees who have the most direct contact with customers feel the most ownership for delivering results customers want.

   b. Reward your longest-tenured customer-facing employees for measurable demonstrations of politeness, empathy, and knowledge in their customer dealings.

   c. Ensure that all the direct reports who work in your unit take responsibility for delivering the results that your company's customers want.

7. You've decided to conduct an audit, one of the listening posts through which companies can learn what products and services customers want and how to better serve customers. Which of the following would you do to conduct the audit?

   a. Be a mystery shopper by visiting one of your company's retail or other business sites and pretending to be a customer.

   b. Gather a large or small informal group of target customers together to test an initial product idea, design, or concept.

   c. Commission a research company to study customer demographics, lifestyles, buying habits, and preferences.

8. To further use listening posts, you decide to initiate a program of follow-up satisfaction calls. What guidelines would you provide the people who would be conducting these calls?

a. Take the opportunity to ask extensive questions about how the customer perceives the company's offerings and service quality.

b. Ask if everything's okay, present a few simple questions about the company's offerings, and provide additional service if needed.

c. Besides asking about and providing service, describe additional offerings the customer may find valuable or interesting.

9. How is the customer value equation expressed?

a. Price plus results, divided by product quality plus promotional investment.

b. Product plus price, divided by promotional effort plus place (distribution channel used).

c. Results plus process quality, divided by price plus access costs.

10. A colleague tells you she's concerned because an order that recently went out to a customer was delivered late, and the product suffered damage during shipment. What might you tell her about recovery from customer-service mistakes?

a. Dissatisfied customers are more likely than others to give feedback about problems and voice complaints directly to the company.

b. Recovering from service mistakes can actually increase customer loyalty and contribute to a company's profitability.

c. Customers who experience creative service recovery tell others less often than those who experience good service the first time.

Answers to test questions

1, b. The three Rs explain why loyal customers are most profitable. Through *retention,* loyal customers continue to buy products. Through *related sales,* they buy new products and services. Through *referrals,* customers praise your company to other people. The three Rs reduce costs, because new sales to existing customers require less marketing, eliminate the hassle of new credit checks, and create less paperwork than selling to new customers. Also, the cost of actually serving and supporting a customer who is familiar with a company and its product lines generally decreases over time.

2, a. Most companies today don't work very hard at developing relationships with long-term customers. Instead, they focus almost all their energy on getting new customers. They mistakenly believe that, to make a profit, they must increase market share. This belief leads to the misguided notion that any customer is a good customer.

3, c. Because target customers highly value your company's offerings, they remain loyal over time. The most successful firms know exactly who their target customers are, focus their energy on creating offerings to please them, and adapt their products and services to meet and exceed these customers' changing expectations.

4, b. Here's how the service-profit chain's mutually reinforcing connections work: When employees have the right skills, support, and rewards, they find their jobs more satisfying. People who enjoy their work become loyal to the company. Loyal employees take time to get to know customers' specific needs and circumstances, creating customer satisfaction and loyalty. And as we've seen, loyal customers are profitable customers.

5, c. Skills can be taught, but it's difficult to train someone to have the right attitude. When you select job candidates for their customer-focused attitude and train them to acquire needed skills, you set the "employee cycle of success" in motion. You complete the success cycle by providing the tools and support employees need to excel, giving them latitude to deliver value to customers, and rewarding them for their contributions to high-quality service.

6, c. Great front-line service—in the form of polite, empathetic, and knowledgeable customer-facing employees—is not enough. *Everyone* in an organization needs to have a customer-focused attitude in order to support the service-profit chain. No one should be exempt, not even workers who spend little or no time in front of customers. For example, a talented software programmer who lacks a customer-focused attitude may delay product releases, annoying customers *and* his teammates. Unhappy customers and employees may defect, breaking the service-profit chain.

7, a. Audits can generate highly objective information about how customer service can be improved. Audits take many forms.

Perhaps the most popular is mystery shopping, whereby someone visits the company's retail or other business sites and acts as a customer; makes calls to customer-service providers; or actually consumes the company's products or services. But be sure to use audits to gather useful information, not to assign blame or punish people for making customer-service mistakes. Otherwise, employees may view auditing as unfair or as a form of spying.

8, b. Follow-up satisfaction calls can help your company spot service-recovery problems before they begin and can reveal more general information about what target customers value or do not value. They can also help establish trust between the company and the customer. However, to avoid annoying the customer, follow-up calls should be brief, take place shortly after the transaction with the customer, and be a sincere effort to ask about and provide service—not to push other products.

9, c. Customers' perceived value of a product or service they've purchased *increases* when (a) they feel the offering generated valuable results and was delivered in a dependable, timely, and pleasant way, and (b) they feel that the price and any costs associated with obtaining the product are reasonable.

10, b. Customers who experience creative service recovery tell others more often than those who experience routinely good service the first time. Thus, companies can increase customer loyalty and profits by finding ways to provide fast, personalized service recovery—and get it right the second time. Successful service companies recover quickly and learn from their mistakes.

To Learn More

Articles

Chase, Richard B., and Sriram Dasu. "Want to Perfect Your Company's Service? Use Behavioral Science." *Harvard Business Review* OnPoint Enhanced Edition, June 2001.

It may seem as if the topic of service management has been exhausted. Legions of scholars and practitioners have applied queuing theory to bank lines, measured response times to the millisecond, and created cults around "delighting the customer." But practitioners haven't carefully considered the underlying psychology of service encounters—the feelings that customers experience during these encounters, feelings often so subtle they probably couldn't be put into words. Fortunately, behavioral science offers new insights into better service management. In this article, the authors translate findings from behavioral-science research into five operating principles: (1) finish strong; (2) get the bad experiences out of the way early; (3) segment the pleasure, combine the pain; (4) build commitment through choice; and (5) give people rituals and stick to them. Ultimately, only one thing really matters in a service encounter—the customer's perception of what occurred. This article will help you engineer your service encounters to enhance your customers' experiences during the process as well as their recollections of the process after it is completed.

Harvard Business School Publishing. "Return on Customer: A Metric for Customer Profitability: An Interview with Martha Rogers." *Balanced Scorecard Report,* January 2006.

With more and more companies chasing a limited pool of customers, smart companies are focusing on customers—how to keep the valuable ones and grow the relationship. Customer relationship management experts Don Peppers and Martha Rogers recently introduced an innovative metric that they believe may be the next great breakthrough concept in customer strategy and business: return on customer. Analogous to the return on investment concept, return on customer is designed to measure the lifetime value of the customer. Rogers speaks with *Balanced Scorecard Report* about why this metric matters.

Jones, Thomas O., and W. Earl Sasser. "Why Satisfied Customers Defect." *Harvard Business Review* OnPoint Enhanced Edition, June 2001.

Most managers rejoice if the majority of customers who respond to customer-satisfaction surveys say they are satisfied. But some of those managers may have a big problem. When most customers are saying they are satisfied but not completely satisfied, they are saying that they are unhappy with some aspect of the product or service. If they have the opportunity, they will defect. Companies that excel in satisfying customers excel both in listening to customers and in interpreting what customers with different levels of satisfaction are telling them.

Nunes, Joseph C., and Xavier Dreze. "Your Loyalty Program Is Betraying You." *Harvard Business Review* OnPoint Enhanced Edition, April 2006.

Even as loyalty programs are launched left and right, many are being scuttled. How can that be? These days, everyone knows that an old customer retained is worth more than a new customer won. What is so hard about making a simple loyalty program work? Quite a lot, the authors say. The biggest challenges include clarifying business goals, engineering the reward structure, and creating incentives powerful enough to change buying behavior but not so generous that they erode margins. Additionally, companies have to sort out the puzzles of consumer psychology, which can result, for example, in two rewards of equal economic value, inspiring very different levels of purchasing. Companies striving to generate customer loyalty should avoid five common mistakes: don't create a new commodity, which can result in price wars and other tit-for-tat competitive moves; don't cater to the disloyal by making rewards easy for just anyone to reap; don't reward purchasing volume over profitability; don't give away the store; and, finally, don't promise what can't be delivered.

Reichheld, Frederick F. "Loyalty-Based Management." *Harvard Business Review* OnPoint Enhanced Edition, November 2000.

Few companies have systematically revamped their operations with customer loyalty in mind. When a company consistently delivers superior value and wins customer loyalty, market share and revenues go up and the cost of acquiring new customers goes down. The company then can pay workers better. Increased pay boosts employee morale and commitment; as employees stay longer, their productivity goes up and training costs fall; employees' overall job satisfaction, combined with their experience, helps them serve customers better; and customers are then more inclined to stay loyal to the company. Finally, as the best customers and employees become part of the loyalty-based system, competitors are left to survive with less desirable customers and less talented employees.

Reinartz, Werner, and Vishesh Kumar. "The Mismanagement of Customer Loyalty," *Harvard Business Review,* July 2002.

Who wouldn't want loyal customers? Surely loyal customers should cost less to serve, they'd be willing to pay more than other customers, and they'd actively market your company by word of mouth, right? Maybe not. Study of the relationship between customer loyalty and profits plumbed from sixteen thousand customers in four companies' databases tells a different story. The authors found that the link between customers and profitability was more complicated because customers fall into four groups, not two. Simply put: not all loyal customers are profitable, and not all profitable customers are loyal. The authors suggest an alternative to traditional tools for segmenting customers, based on well-established "event-history modeling" techniques that more accurately predict future buying probabilities. Armed with such a tool, marketers can correctly identify which customers belong in which category and market accordingly.

Books

Blattberg, Robert C., Gary Getz, and Jacquelyn S. Thomas. *Customer Equity: Building and Managing Relationships as Valuable Assets.* Boston: Harvard Business School Press, 2001.

> What's a customer worth? The company that can answer this question precisely is the company with an edge in the customer-based, technology- and information-intensive economy of today. But how can an asset as intangible as customer value be measured? This book provides a solution: a fully developed, highly practical new marketing system for measuring and managing customer value as a financial asset— a system uniquely suited to today's rapidly changing, increasingly digital marketplace.

Harvard Business School Publishing. *The Manager's Guide to Communicating with Customers. Harvard Management Communication Letter* Collection. Boston: Harvard Business School Publishing, 2001.

> This *Harvard Management Communication Letter* resource collection contains the following seven articles:
>
> - "Are You Reaching Your Customers?"
> - "Communicating with Your Customers on the Web"
> - "Connecting with Your Customers"
> - "Mapping the Frontiers of E-Mail Marketing"
> - "The Secrets and Science of Direct-Mail Marketing"

- "Zeroing in on What Customers Really Want"

- "Zyman on Marketing"

Heil, Gary, Tom Parker, Deborah C. Stephen, and Jan Carlzon. *One Size Fits One: Building Relationships One Customer and One Employee at a Time.* New York: John Wiley & Sons, 1999.

The authors show how to instill a commitment to quality service throughout the organization by establishing a companywide program of continuous service improvement, eliminating ineffective management practices, and creating a sense of accountability for quality service in every employee.

Nunes, Paul F., and Brian Johnson. *Mass Affluence: Seven New Rules of Marketing to Today's Consumer.* Boston: Harvard Business School Press, 2004.

Mass marketing is back, say Paul Nunes and Brian Johnson—but with a new target and a fresh approach that companies ignore at their peril. Whereas the mass marketing concepts of the 1950s consisted of lowest common denominator strategies aimed at the "middle class," Nunes and Johnson argue that the rules of mass marketing must be rewritten to appeal to today's burgeoning mass of different—and far more affluent—consumers. The "moneyed masses" have more disposable income than ever, and research shows the richest among them are not spending up to their potential—thus creating a windfall of opportunity for marketers. Based on extensive consumer research, *Mass Affluence* outlines seven new rules for capturing this largely ignored market.

eLearning

Harvard Business School Publishing. *Case in Point*. Boston: Harvard Business School Publishing, 2004.

Case in Point is a flexible set of online cases, designed to help prepare middle- and senior-level managers for a variety of leadership challenges. These short, reality-based scenarios provide sophisticated content to create a focused view into the realities of the life of a leader. Your managers will experience: Aligning Strategy, Removing Implementation Barriers, Overseeing Change, Anticipating Risk, Ethical Decisions, Building a Business Case, Cultivating Customer Loyalty, Emotional Intelligence, Developing a Global Perspective, Fostering Innovation, Defining Problems, Selecting Solutions, Managing Difficult Interactions, The Coach's Role, Delegating for Growth, Managing Creativity, Influencing Others, Managing Performance, Providing Feedback, and Retaining Talent.

Harvard Business School Publishing. *Service Success*. Boston: Harvard Business School Publishing, 2003.

Developing excellent service relationships is key to attracting and retaining customers. However, providing good service goes beyond interacting pleasantly with customers. The "service-profit chain" is a framework that demonstrates how loyal employees and satisfied customers can lead to substantial growth for an organization. *Service Success* places strong emphasis on the impact a manager can have on developing employees, improving service capability, and ultimately, contributing to an organization's bottom line. *Service Success* is based on the research and analysis by the Harvard Business School Service Management Group, including professors James Heskett and Jeffrey Rayport, and developed from proven and reliable content. It is based on seminal research by multiple HBS and other experts in the field of business communications and includes twenty-three *Harvard Business Review* articles as resources.

Sources for Focusing on Your Customer

The following sources aided in development of this book:

Duran, Nicole. "Airlines Change to Better Service." *South Bend Tribune,* October 14, 1999.

———. "United Airlines Dumps Feeder for Air Wisconsin." *South Bend Tribune,* November 18, 1999.

Heskett, James L., Thomas O. Jones, Gary W. Loveman, W. Earl Sasser Jr., and Leonard A. Schlesinger. "Putting the Service-Profit Chain to Work." *Harvard Business Review,* March–April 1994.

Heskett, James L., and Jeffrey Rayport. "Breakthrough Service Management." An Interactive Internet Course. Module 3: Building Loyalty. San Francisco: Pensare, and Boston: Harvard Business School Publishing, 1999.

Heskett, James L., W. Earl Sasser Jr., and Leonard A. Schlesinger. *The Service-Profit Chain: How Leading Companies Link Profit and Growth to Loyalty, Satisfaction and Value.* New York: The Free Press, 1997.

How to Really Deliver Superior Customer Service. 2nd ed. Boston: *Inc.* magazine, 1996.

Reichheld, Frederick F. An interview in *Management Science,* March 1997.

———. "Loyalty-Based Management." *Harvard Business Review,* March–April 1993.

Reichheld, Frederick F., and W. Earl Sasser Jr. "Zero Defections— Quality Comes to Services." *Harvard Business Review,* September–October 1990.

Service Success. The Interactive Manager Series. An interactive CD-ROM. Boston: Harvard Business School Publishing, 1998.

Sewell, Carl, and Paul B. Brown. *Customers for Life: How to Turn That One-Time Buyer Into a Lifetime Customer.* New York: Currency, 1998.

Notes

Notes

Notes

Notes

Notes

Notes

Notes

Notes

Notes

How to Order

Harvard Business School Press publications are available worldwide from your local bookseller or online retailer.

You can also call:
1-800-668-6780

Our product consultants are available to help you 8:00 a.m.–6:00 p.m., Monday–Friday, Eastern Time. Outside the U.S. and Canada, call: 617-783-7450.

Please call about special discounts for quantities greater than ten.

You can order online at:
www.HBSPress.org